"Do not worry about anything,
but in everything by prayer
and supplication with
thanksgiving let your requests
be made known to God.
And the peace of God, which
surpasses all understanding,
will guard your hearts and
your minds in Christ Jesus."

-philippians 4:6-7

D1158857

UPs
AND
downs

Prayers
By and
4 Teens

Prayers compiled and arranged by
Elizabeth Halfmann

Liguori
ONE LIGUORI DRIVE
LIGUORI MO 63057-9999

Imprimi Potest:
Thomas D. Picton, C.Ss.R.
Provincial, Denver Province
The Redemptorists

Published by Liguori Publications
Liguori, Missouri 63057-9999

Library of Congress Cataloging-in-Publication Data

Ups & downs : prayers by & 4 teens : prayers / compiled and arranged by
Elizabeth Halfmann.—1st ed.
    p. cm.
  ISBN 978-0-7648-1882-0
  1. Catholic teenagers—Prayers and devotions. 2. Catholic Church—
Prayers and devotions. I. Halfmann, Elizabeth. II. Title: Ups and downs.
  BX2150.U77 2010
  242'.63—dc22

                                                          2010002754

Scripture citations are taken from the New Revised Standard Version of the
Bible, copyright 1989 by the Division of Christian Education of the National
Council of the Churches of Christ in the USA. All rights reserved. Used with
permission.

Liguori Publications, a nonprofit corporation, is an apostolate of the Redemptorists. To learn more about the Redemptorists, visit Redemptorists.com.

To order, call 800-325-9521
www.liguori.org

Printed in the United States of America
14 13 12 11 10   5 4 3 2 1
First Edition

Contents

Dedication

For all those hearts yearning for Full Life,
seeking the Truth, or praying for God's way...
may you find peace in these words,
united in prayer.

Acknowledgments

To all who have shared and submitted their stories, prayers, and reflections within these pages, know of my (and God's) deep gratitude and joy for you.

And

To all of my family and friends who've supported me through prayers, assistance in vetting, and help in formatting along the way, especially Kirsten Antonacci, Miles Dierker, Samantha Halfmann, Kevin Damazyn, Katie Potter, Samantha Doherty, Maria Sciaroni, Timm Chauvin, Courtney Campbell, Stephen Brinkmeyer, Kay and Paul Halfmann, and so many more:

"Faithful friends are life-saving medicine;
    and those who fear the Lord will find them.
Those who fear the Lord direct
    their friendship aright,
    for as they are, so are their neighbors also."
                                            –Sirach 6:16–17

Most of all, my dear Jesus, I could not have done this without the inspiration of your Holy Spirit and your Father's guidance. From the depths of my heart, I thank you.

"Let no one despise your youth,
but set the believers an example in speech and
conduct, in love, in faith, and in purity."

–1 Timothy 4:12

Foreword

Every day, we hear many, many voices. Many of these voices try to turn us from God, the one voice of truth, who so longs to speak to our hearts. The words that fill these pages cry out to God, praise him, and show a yearning to know God, the one **true** voice, and express a desire to enter into a relationship with him.

As teenagers, we are filled with desires. We desire happiness, success, solutions to problems, and, at the base of it all, **love**. We will often go to any crazy length to find these things and make them our own. When we don't find these things, though, when our lives fill with brokenness and pain, instead of satisfaction and strength, we are frustrated and feel utterly let down. Sometimes our brokenness stems from hurt in the past from a death, break up, or abuse. At other times, our pain is more immediate, caused by gossip and drama, endless questioning, and mask-wearing. As our pain increases, our hearts shatter within our very selves. And the worst part is that (if we try to keep it hidden) no one else may ever know about the hurt. But as we try to keep and mend our hearts, our primary desire for love intensifies.

Though we don't necessarily feel this broken every second, whether it's a good day or a bad day, let's be honest: life is not easy. There's homework, and relationship struggles, and fights about driving privileges, and practices or rehearsals, and school, and youth group, and family parties no one really wants to attend. Regardless of what any adult might say, we really are busy, busy people! Sometimes it's impossible to even sit back and understand our own feelings. The mystery and beauty in this is God's presence through our crazy schedules. Though sometimes we may be moving too fast to realize it, God wants to enter into our daily routines and he strengthens our desire for pure love through our busyness.

All of our searching and desiring for love can only be fulfilled through God, who **is** Love. He wants to be the voice who reaches through all of our life's chaos and pulls us through to him. Through surrendering our questions and our busy lives to him, we begin to find answers and take time to develop a true friendship with God as Father, Son, and Holy Spirit. The more we delve into this relationship, the more our desire to participate in the love of God grows. The other voices that remind us of our brokenness are silenced by the compassionate blood of christ that pours over our wounds to heal us. when we look to fulfill our desire for love in a speaking-listening relationship with god himself through prayer, our hearts cannot be disappointed. living in the love of god opens us to praying daily, praying constantly, and attempting to live life as a prayer in our own unique ways. our lives begin to look different because the bond of prayer unites us to god.

As we begin, continue, or come back to our relationship with god, the holy spirit puts the fire of love in our hearts for which we thirst most. god, who is love, calls us to more. he calls us to full communion with him through his grace, which in turn affects the concrete ways we live our lives in faith, hope, and love. he has always stayed by our sides, even in times of doubt, confusion, or hurt. Now, when we fully unite our hearts to his, we realize **his desire for us to live fully in his love**.

Even when we live lives of prayer, not every day on our journey as christians is going to be easy. Relationships take a lot of work. Many days, truthfully, are going to be quite hard. However, it is in those tough moments that god opens his great Arms of love to us because he desires our hearts so badly. My prayer is that all who pray the words in this book will be united in their desire for God's love and experience the fulfillment of him as Love in their everyday lives. God desires to hear **your** voice; listen to **his** in your weakest moments, your strongest moments, and every instant in between. He loves you.

—Liz Halfmann

Searching & Questioning

A man named Albert Camus, a French author and philosopher, once said, "You will never be happy if you continue to search for what happiness consists of. You will never live if you are looking for the meaning of life." What happens, then, when we hit a wall? When we feel that we cannot go on living because we don't know our objective in life? We search for a purpose, for an answer to our questions. In our darkest times we turn to the light, to a God who has always been waiting in the background but is sometimes ignored in the hustle and bustle of our hectic lives.

So that's it, problem solved.

Right?

Wrong.

Unfortunately the answer is not that easy. In fact, there isn't only one answer to the many complex questions we have. We want to know the reasons for our lives and troubles, our relationships, our losses, and our misunderstandings of the world around us. Contrary to popular belief, it is not wrong to question our lives, our beliefs, or even our God. Everyone reaches a turning point or crossroads in life and faith. Naturally, we fear both choice and change. However, if you aren't careful in the search for your wants and beliefs, you can lose yourself.

From personal experience I've found that such a predicament can interfere with the lives of even the most confident investors in faith.

No one is immune to the confusion and curiosity that comes with the package of being a teenager. I have also learned that, much to my annoyance, the one thing I'm searching for usually presents itself the second I stop looking. So although it may be the most difficult thing to do, stepping back and taking a deep breath may be the best thing for a searching soul. Every situation is different along with every personality. One person's pursuit of happiness will not lead them along the same path as someone else's because there is no set path!

We have been told for years that God is always there for us. All you have to do is turn around, open your eyes, and he's there. Right? Of course these things are never that easy, especially for us teenagers. He **is** always there, but sometimes we just can't see him. We get so lost in what we want that we forget God is even there. We also forget that he doesn't like to be shoved in a box and thrown into the back of our cluttered closet of life.

So, clean out your closet! Get out of the habit of piling up all your thoughts, questions, and prayers. Don't give up when you hit a wall; it happens to everyone! Learn how to bounce back and you'll be able to handle anything life throws at you. God will never run away. He will always be right behind you, waiting patiently for you to open your eyes.

"He who has a why to live can bear almost any how."–Friedrich Nietzsche

—Hayley Osman

God,

Take my hands.
Place them where you will.
I am lost, yet all I know
and trust lies in you.

I offer up my weaknesses,
my sins, my stress, my pains.
Mold me, God, into
something beautiful.

I long to serve you,
though I fail so much;
so now I will just
listen, because I am so lost.

—S. Blackwell

Lord,
Every day is a challenge.
Guide me to the right path and let me know
I can always rely on you.

I need your guidance the most right now.
All of my decisions will make a difference
in the future.

Amen

—M. Pedraja

"For surely I know the plans I have for you,
says the Lord, plans for your welfare and not
for harm, to give you a future with hope.
Then when you call upon me and come and pray
to me, I will hear you. When you search for me,
you will find me; if you seek me with all your
heart, I will let you find me, says the Lord..."

—Jeremiah 29:11-14

I really wonder when people say
that they believe in God because he
is always there whenever they
have a problem. How do we
know whether he is there
for us or not? we've never
seen him before and we
do not even know what
he looks like. yet, if he is
there, is he there for non-christians as well?
I am not christian, but people say that God is
always watching me and loving me. I know God
is good to me and he has given me unbelievable
gifts: I have a wonderful family and I came to
America. I have tried to believe what the Bible
says and in the existence of God. Nevertheless,
I still doubt him. sometimes, I am jealous of those
who have faith in God.

—S.H.

✝ ✝ ✝

Jesus, my heart aches for you.
I don't know what to do.
I love you so much and yet I'm so afraid.
Please help me, Lord.

—E. wicks

"'Ask, and it will be given you;
search, and you will find;
knock, and the door will be opened for you.
For everyone who asks receives,
and everyone who searches finds,
and for everyone who knocks,
the door will be opened.'"

—matthew 7:7–8

God of justice and truth,
why do evildoers prey upon the innocent
and attack the pure and defenseless?
My heart goes out to the oppressed,
but by myself, what can I do?
without your grace, what can I accomplish?
Help me to defend those who abide by your laws.
Bless me with fortitude.
I know that you will not abandon me,
but will replace my uncertainty with courage.
You shall rescue all who believe in you,
and songs of your glory will resound
through the skies.
You, Lord, are the God of Redemption!
Amen.

—L. Williams

✝ ✝ ✝

*"But strive first for the kingdom of God
and his righteousness, and all these things
will be given to you as well."*

—Matthew 6:33

who?

вe careful to judge
who you think you see
before you realize
who really is she.

she is the speaker and listener.
she is the helper and the helped.
she is the betrayer and the betrayed.

she wants to grow up and to be a child.
she wants to hide and to be known.
she wants to trust and to be trusted,
wants to love and to be loved.

she's broken and strong.
she's naïve but mature.
she's quiet but her head is spinning
with thoughts,
with songs,
with prayers.

what you think you see
isn't really she.
she is you,
she is me.
нe is she.

—F. нeumann

I always thought searching was so hard. Then
I discovered when I let God do the searching
for me, I always end up finding what I didn't
know I was looking for.

—L. Heath

✝ ✝ ✝

Jesus, when will I ever conceive of your plan
    for me?
God, who is it that you truly want me to be?
I am so confused, and I get misled.
I disappoint you continuously.
These stupid voices in my head
guide me away from your reality.
I need you, Lord,
more now than ever.
I need to stop doubting you,
and remember
your love is forever.
So what is it that I'm missing?
I know there is something. I just can't
    pinpoint it.
So many people I see can trust you,
but I have a hard time.
Lord, I need help.
I need faith.

—A. Doerr

"Humbly ask God to increase your faith. And then, with new lights, you will fully appreciate the difference between the paths of the world and your way as an apostle."

From *The Way*
by Saint Josemaria Escriva

In Mary's Shoes

Kneeling on the ground,
feeling as if you will pass out.
"Pregnant?
What?
Me?
How could this be?"
The glowing figure asks if you will accept.
You do, for it is God's will.
And you should most definitely obey.

Then in the back of your mind,
you think of the husband
that your daddy assigned.
"Holy cow!
I ruined his life.
We were supposed to be
man and wife.
There is no way on earth
that he will accept this child and I.
He will think this whole Jesus thing
is just one big lie."

You run to your cousin Elizabeth,
hoping she will not object to the truth,
for the angel told you
she shall bear fruit, too.
You embrace,
and are too afraid

to go back to your home place.
so you stay with your cousin
for a month or two,
then go back to your hometown,
for it is what you feel you should do.

Fear fills you
when you must confront your husband-to-be.
Your pregnancy is obvious.
He will think you were with
another man.
Hopefully he will understand
God's enormous plan.
He cannot believe it at first.
You cry to his feet
and tell him
it is what God wants you to do.

surprisingly,
the next day
he tells you that he loves you
and will help you through it all.
what caused this sudden change of heart?
Did he get God's call?
Did he see the angel too?
He has heard of God's plan,
and realized
that for it to be carried out,
you must bear the christ child in your womb.
some might call it an obstacle,

but you consider it
a wonderful compliment or gift
from the Lord.
He is the greatest gift that will ever be, in fact.
you sit in the marketplace
and wonder in disbelief
why God has chosen
you.

—A. Doerr

✝ ✝ ✝

I didn't promise things would be easy.
I just promised to help you.

I didn't promise that you wouldn't ever feel alone.
I just promised you wouldn't be.

—F. Heumann

o Lord, I see you all around me, and
I see all the beautiful things you've created,
but for some reason...
I can't find you...
I feel like you've abandoned me.
I need you to come back to me.
I trust that you will,
and that soon I will realize that you never left.
I trust that you will always be there for me.
I trust that even when I turn my back on you,
you will always be there for me.
Lord, please help me come back to you,
so that I can experience your glory once again.
oh Glorious God, help me.
Amen.

—M. Heitkamp

✝ ✝ ✝

"Can a woman forget her nursing child,
    or show no compassion
    for the child of her womb?
Even these may forget,
    yet I will not forget you.
See, I have inscribed you
    on the palms of my hands ..."

—Isaiah 49:15–16

Now every year his parents went to Jerusalem for the festival of the Passover. And when he was twelve years old, they went up as usual for the festival. When the festival was ended and they started to return, the boy Jesus stayed behind in Jerusalem, but his parents did not know it. Assuming that he was in the group of travelers, they went a day's journey. Then they started to look for him among their relatives and friends. When they did not find him, they returned to Jerusalem to search for him. After three days they found him in the temple, sitting among the teachers, listening to them and asking them questions. And all who heard him were amazed at his understanding and his answers. When his parents saw him they were astonished; and his mother said to him, "Child, why have you treated us like this? Look, your father and I have been searching for you in great anxiety." He said to them, "Why were you searching for me? Did you not know that I must be in my Father's house?"

—Luke 2:41-49

I don't know what is wrong with me, Jesus. I cannot concentrate during prayer and during church I feel like I'm antsy and I need to leave. Lord, it is getting so hard for me to trust in you and to give up myself. I don't know why exactly. It's getting so hard to believe that you're really there, that you actually are.

I know that this is a trial I've been sent or that I'm putting myself through, so I ask you to help me through it. Please, remember that though my mind falters on the journey, my heart is eternally set on you. Grant me the strength to accept your graces, especially when they come in the form of trials!

—E. Wicks

"Likewise the Spirit helps us in our weakness;
for we do not know how to pray as we ought,
but the very Spirit intercedes with sighs
    too deep for words.
And God, who searches the heart,
knows what is the mind of the Spirit,
because the Spirit intercedes for the saints
according to the will of God."

—Romans 8:26–27

✝ ✝ ✝

"Be still, and know that I am God!"

—Psalm 46:11

✝ ✝ ✝

I don't know how to love you anymore
or how to pray. So, let me stand stone still,
and speak no words but merely be
in your presence.

—E. Wicks

Lighted Highway

His eyes shone on the road
Light highway to the clouds, to the sky
The cross at the end called to me
The other road full of darkness
A dark alley of alcoholism and addiction
My friends called to me at the end
who should i choose?

His eyes were full of tears
Not from the pain of his hands,
    but the pain of my doubts
he called my name, he called out my thoughts,
    even my flaws
He called to me to say i love you

My friends are getting drunk
Looking for the next great buzz
They called "we are having such a blast
come hang out with us"
who should i choose?

i walked down the path full of light
i chose the path of love
i chose the true path.
i walked determinedly to the cross
opening my arms
to him

—c. jump

Wounded Hearts

Life. It is something we all have in common, along with the fact that we all encounter hardships. We all encounter unique hardships, though: addiction, depression, death of close friends and loved ones, and—one that for many can be the hardest—the dark night of faith. These nights, we lay awake and feel nothing spiritually; these times, we feel broken, useless, and unfixable. These are nights when we question whether God is really working in our lives, times when we question if he truly still loves us. Nights such as this can shake the very foundation of our faith, and for some, can lead to giving up on God. These times of extreme desolation are tough times. Finding the strength and patience to make it through can be hard, but these virtues can only come from God.

In times of desolation, the very times when it feels like God has abandoned you, when you are spiritually dry and feel very little or nothing at all, the **truth** is that God has **not** abandoned you; he has **not** given up on loving you. The "dark night" of faith is a time when satan and his evil spirits are attempting to destroy the beautiful relationship you have with the Father that keeps you from falling into the devil's snares. Remembering your relationship with God and his unconditional love, love revealed through the cross and the death of God's son, Jesus, can help you continue to know and trust in him. Using this knowledge and trust can help you gain two things that will help you make it out of the dark night and into the glorious light of day once again.

The transformation from desolation to the consolation of faith begins when you embrace the patience and perseverance that flows from God, and focus on the knowledge that he has not given up on you. God still loves you and cares for you, and he created you beautifully with his whole heart. Overcoming your brokenness can be a hard task and can spiritually and emotionally exhaust you, but it comes down to the fact that with God you can. "They shall run and not be weary, they shall walk and not faint." (Isaiah 40:31) This is an awesome Bible verse, and if you are experiencing the dark night of faith, I encourage you to memorize this verse, keep it on your mind, and remember it always. Believe in it and trust it. Trust that God still loves you and has not abandoned you; know that it is through your self-surrender and your struggles that you come to find that trust. As you begin to step back and let go of trying to control your own lives, if you allow God to take over, you can allow his will to be done.

I pray that these words, which have flowed from the Father to you through these prayers, speak to you in a way that brings you hope for the future...

—Miles Dierker

down in the dumps, under the dirt, covered
in everything, messing up, trying to forget,
wanting to be clean, struggling within, and
making a scene.

needing guidance and a way back on track,
trying not to turn her back, she wants to stand
tall, but feels oh so small.

wanting a way to feel alright again, she starts
talking to God as a way to begin.

—P. Dowler

god,
i just don't feel good and i'm having a bad day.
you must be speaking to me through the kind
and loving people around me.
But do i notice? no.
do i listen? no.
why?
Because all i care about right now is me
and my bad day.
i am trying to get through it but not really
turning to you for the solution.
i love you and know you are here for me;
please send me reminders of that love every day.
Help me to listen to you
with my whole mind and heart,
and to pray until something happens.
only then may i find true peace within you
and get on track to feeling better and
being a happier person.

—J. winkelmann

Hey there God,

I've been feeling pretty crummy lately. I feel useless, voiceless, ugly, stupid, and hopeless. It's hard for me to see the point. Life is so overwhelming. I know I shouldn't turn to suicide, drinking, or eating disorders, but to be honest, those are tempting choices. I know those choices will only make life worse. I've seen how they have hurt friends. Help me to see my gifts and blessings. I need some strength back. I want to feel life again. Thanks for listening, God.

—T. Kelly

I feel like a tree, God. I am the tree and I am all the branches, holding and helping the leaves at the end of them—my friends. But these leaves keep changing colors and dying and falling off, away from our friendship. And it seems that there is someone at the bottom of the tree with an axe just trying to cut me down and shred me to pieces, chopping at me. I feel like if I just stop and surrender it all, all the leaves will fall and die—my friendships will all be gone.

—S. Halfmann

How long, O Lord?
Will you forget me
forever?
How long will you hide your face from me?
How long must I bear pain in my soul,
and have sorrow in my heart all day long?
How long shall my enemy be exalted over me?
Consider and answer me, O Lord my God!

—Psalm 13:1-3

God,

In times like these, I don't feel good enough. I feel hardly worthy of your love and praise. I have let others define me, rank me, judge me. But they are not at fault for my sadness, Lord, only me. I have lost sight of my self-worth that you gave me. I have allowed myself to drown in others' opinions and forgotten the only one that truly matters: yours.

Lord, send me courage to love the person you love. Send me the humility to never tempt others to lose sight of your love for them. And, Lord, finally, send me the faith to know that I am good enough for you, which is all that matters.

Amen.

—A. christian

✝ ✝ ✝

Lord,

Please look out for all those who suffer from low self-esteem. Help them to realize how much they are loved by you. Comfort them when times get rough, and help them to trust in your plan for them, so that they may soon find peace and comfort in the body you gave them.

Amen.

—A. schwent

"*God saw everything that he had made,
and indeed, he found it very good.*"

—Genesis 1:31

✝ ✝ ✝

"*. . . you are precious in my sight,
and honored, and I love you.*"

—Isaiah 43:4

<u>verse 1</u>: I let you control me, did what you told me and all I got was a slap in the face. Mistaken for my best friend, said you'd be there till the end. But when I try to be myself, you find a friend in someone else. I try and try to be like you but no one ever knew I would hide.

<u>chorus</u>: Behind my disguise, all these people's dirty looks and lies. Should I try just to be what you want and try to hide behind my disguise?

<u>verse 2</u>: He says he loves me and I bought it. I've never felt love like this before. All his smooth talking makes my heart melt into his words. But once I gave him all of me, he leaves me out to dry, never really seeing the pain I feel inside.

<u>chorus</u>: Behind my disguise, all these people's dirty looks and lies. Should I try just to be what you want and try to hide behind my disguise?

<u>verse 3</u>: I'm about to fall, about to give it all, about to give up and take my life away. I can't do this; I'm through with this. Take my blade and slit my wrists to take the pain away. But you step in and show me your love and tell me everything's going to be OK.

<u>verse 4</u>: No more disguise because God is with me; he saved me from all the looks and lies. I don't have to try to be what I'm not and I will never have to lie again. He loves me just the way I am and I will never have to hide behind a disguise.

—B. Campos

I've seen the scars on your arms.
I've seen the pain and anger and hurt in your eyes.
I was there for the tears flowing all night.
I felt the guilt and shame with and without you.
I shook off the lies.
I've been scared out of my mind.
I've waited staring at the doors...
    eyeing the telephone...watching the screen.

we've made the list.
we've talked about it.

But somewhere, deep inside, the pain remained.
The sadness lingered.
The fake face was always there
    for those who didn't know.
The edge was so close.
And yet it was still in me...the anger...the guilt.
No matter how hard I tried...to surrender...
    I could never fully.
I wept inside both day and night.
I quivered in the closet, on the phone,
    on the computer.
And yet it stayed with me
because of the lie.
one simple manipulation
until I came clean.

And then I felt you, God.
I felt the love.
I felt guilt-free.

we forgave.
we were forgiven.

But I will never forget it,
that Tuesday walk,
that day in my room,
that saturday drive,
the late-night worries that kept me up,
the tears that weighed me down inside
    that would not come out.
Now I am numb.

God saved me.
You, God, you brought me out of the lowest of lows.
You put my smile back on my face,
    though forever changed.

—S. Halfmann

Give Me Strength

she cried the day she had to watch her momma
   go away.
The tears fell down her face,
   cuz she's stuck in yesterday.
when everything was perfect,
   and things were still OK.
Now her world is ruined,
   so she hits her knees and prays.
And she says,
"please, Lord, give me strength to make it
   to tomorrow, cuz I'm not sure 'bout today.
   I know there's bumps along the way.
   But I'm sure as long as you're here I'm okay.
   so give me strength."

The proof is there, you can see her pain is real.
still you never know just how she feels.
As the world is closing in, she looks to the sky.
And she knows she'll be alright.
And she says,
"please, Lord, give me strength to make it
    to tomorrow, cuz I'm not sure 'bout today.
    I know there's bumps along the way.
    But I'm sure as long as you're here I'm okay.
    so give me strength."
Now that girl is grown, in her mind and in her soul.
she happily prays to the Lord. And she says,
"You, Lord, you gave me strength. I made it
    through tomorrows when I wasn't sure
    'bout todays. oh, I saw bumps along the way,
    but you stayed right beside me, and made
    everything okay. You gave me strength.
"yeah; you gave me strength.
    And everything's okay."

—M. zimmerman

Turn it up loud and you can hear the silence,
the emptiness, the sadness.
I'm surrounded by people,
but I feel so alone,
don't know which direction to go.
The choice remains,
but I'm lost for words.
Give me your strength.
Be my rock, my guide, my God.

—L. Halfmann

✝ ✝ ✝

"Jesus said . . . 'Do not fear, only believe.'"

—Mark 5:36

✝ ✝ ✝

Before & After

The world is getting darker,
Blackness tightening all around me,
Fumbling blindly through the shadows,
Until you came along and found me

and showed me that my eyes were closed.

—A. Moser

*"Cast all your anxiety on him,
because he cares for you."*

—1 peter 5:7

✝ ✝ ✝

*As he walked along, he saw a man blind from
birth. His disciples asked him, "Rabbi, who
sinned, this man or his parents, that he was
born blind?" Jesus answered, "Neither this man
nor his parents sinned; he was born blind so
that God's works might be revealed in him. We
must work the works of him who sent me while
it is day; night is coming when no one can work.
As long as I am in the world, I am the light of
the world." When he had said this, he spat on
the ground and made mud with the saliva and
spread the mud on the man's eyes, saying to
him, "Go, wash in the pool of Silo'am" (which
means Sent). Then he went and washed and
came back able to see.
He said, "Lord, I believe." And he worshiped
him. Jesus said, "I came into this world for
judgment so that those who do not see may see,
and those who do see may become blind."*

—John 9:1-7, 38-39

Take my fear, unmask me.
Release this pain and set me free.

—P. Dowler

✝ ✝ ✝

O Jesus, keep all temptations away from me!
I am so very weak and cannot take much more.

—J. Ecle

✝ ✝ ✝

*Jesus prayed, "My Father, if it is possible,
let this cup pass from me;
yet not what I want but what you want."*

—Matthew 26:39

✝ ✝ ✝

Lord,

Lay me down in this brokenness. Take from my
life what isn't holy, the small things around me,
or even life itself. If it is not meant for me, take
it away. In this life I claim nothing but my sin as
mine. Wash away the mud and dirt that sin has
cast upon me. Bandage my wounds and heal my
life...Jesus...I need you...all glory to the King,
past, present, and future.

Amen.

—M. Dierker

I lay down in my brokenness
Take away what's not holiness
I lay down in my brokenness
wash away all my, wash away all my sin
wash away all my sin

And I lay me down
you wear the crown
And I lay me down
you wear the crown

show me your face!
Loving embrace

o I lay me down

—Pete Buncher, "I Lay Me Down"
© 2009, Pete Buncher

the nails in his hands are the nails that hold
    my tethered and sinful heart together
there are two halves: the world half,
    so evil and misleading, and
the other, his kingdom, extending beyond the
    farthest cloud in the vast blue sky
only his love can mend my brokenness
when the world is at its best my heart is
    at its worst
the temple in which he dwells is burdened
it is no longer a pleasing place for him to be
so i wander... sometimes for what seems like
    40 days and nights
he never leaves me orphaned; however,
    i am still blinded by the light
then, as if a miracle is blossoming,
    light penetrates the atmosphere and
    warms my skin
now his kingdom is at its best

i am renewed
i've been set free from my pain
i release it from within like rain
it collects in my eyes and pours down,
    never ceasing
for as the nails pierced him, he cleansed me
tears drip now only in gratitude
    for what he has given up for me
what greater love is there than he?

—P. Dowler

✝ ✝ ✝

"'Death has been swallowed up in victory.
Where, O death, is your victory?
Where, O death, is your sting?'"

—1 corinthians 15:54–55

Fight or surrender

Hoping to meet my savior
But fighting for my killer
The killer who stains my white robe
Is it me or is it him?

should I fight or should I surrender?

yet, my savior still waits for my hand
He still loves me
savior, please help me get up
Please stop me from betraying you again
My heart belongs to you not my murderer

yet I think to myself
should I fight or should I surrender?

I confess to you now
I have sinned and have fought to sin
I have seen the answers
And I want to retire in your arms

How beautiful you are
How merciful
I'll only fight for you my savior
I'll eat and drink the life you have given me
I'll surrender to you
And fight for you

—A. Irula

*Finally, be strong in the Lord and
in the strength of his power.
Put on the whole armor of God,
so that you may be able to stand
against the wiles of the devil.
Therefore take up the whole armor of God,
so that you may be able to withstand
on that evil day, and having done everything,
to stand firm.*

—Ephesians 6:10–11, 13

† † †

*"The Lord will fight for you,
and you have only to keep still."*

—Exodus 14:14

christ, your heart is so real because you came
to earth and showed us that you love us enough
to suffer on a tree and be crucified. Lord, they
tortured and beat you and you took every whip
and every ridicule they gave to you. while that
was happening, you were thinking of me. you
thought of me while you were hanging upon that
cross. you forgave your tormentors' sins just
like you have forgiven my sins, just because
I don't know what I am doing, Lord.

your mercy is so abundant, and I ask that this
mercy be poured into my soul and heart. please
pour it into the souls of all those who are far
from you. Allow love to burst out of my heart
just like your heart is exposed to me. Every day
allow my heart to trust in you, and allow it to
burn like a million stars for you and only you.

—B. verhoff

✝ ✝ ✝

*"We know that all things work together
for good for those who love God,
who are called according to his purpose."*

—romans 8:28

41

Hanging On

L ife as a high school student can be tough. Many days I feel trapped in a room where I cannot breathe. As the years in high school go by, I constantly find my busy weeks filled with big tests, quickly approaching deadlines, and heavy expectations to meet. on one particularly stressful day in my junior year, it was barely 10:00 AM and I was already near meltdown. My heart was beating a million miles a minute, my mind was racing around during U.S. history class, my soul silently crying out, "Jesus, Jesus!"

With the accumulation of stress in the average teen's life, it's hard enough to maintain a solid focus on the right priorities and achieve a balance. As high school students, our lives are already complicated, but as christians, our lives are incredibly difficult. sometimes we get distracted by the wrong activities; sometimes we are tested with temptations. I used to ask myself, how in the world is anyone expected to handle all of this?

After much frustration, I found a solution. I take a deep breath and detach myself from the world just for a few minutes, and I dedicate my whole heart, mind, and soul to Jesus. I place everything in the Lord's hands, where I know that everything will be taken care of. God always has a way of letting me know everything will turn out fine. I contemplate this further, and I envision the cross. I see a man who was stripped of his garments, who was ridiculed by his own people, who gave up his life—for me, for all. My burdens are inconsequential compared to the weight of the whole world's sin.

From Jesus, I find the strength to endure. If we learn to focus our lives on our loving Father's son, we will find strength, as we understand that suffering makes us more like Jesus, who conquered death. I look back at my life, and I no longer see all my stress. Instead, it is clear that my life is full of God's blessings: wonderful family and friends, music that moves my soul, and most importantly, God's amazing, neverending love. And because of that love, I find the spirit to move on and never give up, no matter how difficult life gets.

Dear, sweet Jesus. Let us never fail to keep you at the center of our lives. May we always strive to give glory to our Father in heaven. Amen.

—Jacqueline Ecle

✝ ✝ ✝

"Therefore, my beloved, be steadfast, immovable, always excelling in the work of the Lord, because you know that in the Lord your labor is not in vain."

—1 Corinthians 15:58

This morning I woke up real early,
and couldn't get out of bed.
I was late getting to school,
and my stomach didn't even get fed.
Then I got to Algebra,
turns out I had a test.
Too bad I didn't study
and left the homework on my desk.
Around noon came lunchtime,
my favorite time of day.
I stood in line at chick-fil-a
and watched the wind take my money away.
I didn't think my day could get much worse,
no, not anymore.
I walked out to my beat-up car,
and saw a scratch along my door.
standing in the parking lot,
I shouted to the sky,
thinking you must be laughing
while I was about to cry.
"God, you think you're really funny!"
I said in a sarcastic tone.
"You must be rolling up in Heaven,"
I shouted with a groan.
I got into my car,
and drove away in fury,
flustered, aggravated, and exhausted,
trying to get home in a hurry.
suddenly a car stopped
right in front of me;

glass and metal flying
and wreckage was all I could see.
It might have been a minor wreck,
but you made me come to see
that even though my day was bad,
I was blessed more than I should be.
Sure, sometimes life is messy
and we have pretty cruddy days,
but in the midst of imperfection
I looked to God and prayed:
"God give me grace and patience,
make my heart like yours.
I want to see through your eyes,
help me to be pure.
Even though I get angry
and want to punch a wall,
help me when I'm hurting
and catch me when I fall.
Make me see your goodness
and your saving grace.
Give me understanding
with your warm embrace.
One more thing, Father,
I don't tell you this enough,
but I want to say I love you,
and thanks for giving me your love."
Amen.

—J. Gonzales

Life at home is complicated,
friendships are fading,
and senior year is stressful.
Father, I hope for contentment.
Lord Jesus, I am yearning for reassurance.
Holy Spirit, I need you.

Amen.

—R. Sugucio

✝ ✝ ✝

Recently, life's been passing by so fast.
Papers, tests, homework. Friends, drama,
family. Work, practices, meetings.
I'm exhausted.
Help me to slow down before I crash.

—L. Halfmann

And can any of you by worrying
add a single hour to your span of life?
If then you are not able to do
so small a thing as that,
why do you worry about the rest?

—Luke 12:25-26

✝ ✝ ✝

God, please help me settle my mind, relax my
body, and free my spirit. Help me take care
of everything I need to take care of, with some
time left for me, and for you. The stress is killing
me and I need a break. I'm grateful for these
experiences that will help me in the future,
and even now, but please, let me be soothed:
mind, body, and soul.

—M. Rodriquez

God, I think you're calling my name,
but I can't quite make it out.
I am just so busy right now.
I need you in my life,
but how do I find you?
where are you hiding?

Mom says you're in the children
who she teaches every day.
Dad says you're in the people
who go to church and pray.
Yet some see you everywhere,
in everything you created.
Please give me their eyes,
the eyes of those who see
through the eyes that are yours.

You're my creator and I love you so.
Please, o please,
let my faith in you grow.
I say these sports and things
get in the way,
but really that's a horrible excuse.

Every minute of my life I can pray!
There never is an instance
when I can't talk to you.
You're always there;
I just need to place my trust in you.
So here I go, Lord,
I'm taking my steps.
I'm giving you my hand,
and I can't wait to see
where you decide to lead me.

—A. Doerr

✝ ✝ ✝

"And whatever you do, in word or deed, do
everything in the name of the Lord Jesus,
giving thanks to God the Father through him."
—Colossians 3:17

Lord, my eyes you gave me,
but I am simply stubborn,
since I insist on keeping them shut,
blinded with my own selfish reasons,
and seeing only what is wrong with the world.

Lord, my feet you gave me,
but I am simply a coward,
since when I see those who hurt you,
I quickly turn to flee,
caring not for you, but only for me.

Lord, my hands you gave me,
but I am simply selfish,
since I always have them yearning,
wanting, wanting what I don't have,
ignoring the blessings you have given me.

Lord, my heart you gave me,
but I never share it with you,
since I only share it with those
    who share their own with me,
only giving when I am receiving,
but never giving for what I received from you.

Lord, your son you gave me,
but I am simply forgetful,
since I never thank you
for sacrificing the son you love,
for the love you have for me.

Lord, your love you gave me,
and life,
and joy,
and hope,
and salvation.
May I learn to understand
that you sustain me.

—M. Policarpio

God, grant us the wisdom and the good hearts to begin seeing you always in our everyday lives.

We know that we get easily distracted by the many luxuries, activities, or even the sour spots of our lives. We often need a little nudge to get back on track. Give us that push we need and please guide us to respond to it positively.

Help us to search for you, and let us strive to make you the center of our lives.

Amen.

—J. winkelmann

I feel inadequate and unprepared to face this challenging circumstance. I feel as though I have no tools to deal with it, no shoulder to cry on, nobody to help me... no oxygen. I feel as though I'm swimming, all alone, and I've lost all my strength. There are no flotation devices to be seen, and I cannot keep treading but it seems it is my only choice, other than a suffocating death. I've relied on many oxygen tanks before: the oxygen of technology, the oxygen of friends, the oxygen of self-pity, the oxygen of impurity, the oxygen of people, the oxygen of music, the oxygen of earthly love. But all the oxygen tanks I've tried always run out and leave me gasping for breath. It's unreal when our oxygen runs out... when our personal source of salvation suddenly and totally runs out and we are left trying to breathe on our own. My last tank has run out. And I'm losing strength, gasping for air. And then I remember... I am not a fish! I was not designed to tread forever. I'm not expected to swim and swim, keeping my head in the water, only coming up for breaths every now and then. I'm reminded to breathe.

This is when I stop and let myself feel weak. I surrender my life, my weaknesses, my sorrows, my doubts and uncertainties to the one and only everlasting oxygen tank. sometimes it takes guzzling up each and every oxygen tank we can find to finally get to the perpetual giver of life. it is when i am feeling all alone, weak, in the middle of a huge ocean, that i find God, my oxygen. instead of lifelessly paddling my pruned feet, i let myself float. when the water levels rise and when the waves overrule my ability to swim, i stop breathing on my own. i give my lungs over to the hope-giving, agape-bearing, never-ending oxygen tank—my Lord Jesus christ. it is he who lets me float. it is he who does not expect me to be a fish. it is he who gives me peace when the storm is too big to handle on my own.

Finally, at a resting peace, things are quieter... much quieter. i am able to feel the true and pure oxygen fill my lungs. i can hear words of encouragement and positivity. it is amazing... this peace, in such a dreadful storm. He gently reminds me of things i've experienced, things i've learned, that can help me cope. i see memories of days and nights when it felt impossible, but how, with his help, i could see clearly. He reminds me of all the other times i was not in control, and how i was able to emerge stronger because i relied on his faithfulness and strength. i am so content knowing i always have oxygen pumping into my heart, whether i'm in a weak, strong, content, scared, confused, tired, sick, silly, lovely, or treacherous state. i love you, my oxygen.

—E. Giannelli

It is the simple things that happen every minute of the day, like a smile, great song, or even a hug that make my day worth living. I pray that God will send us reminders of his love and that we all may recognize them. I thank God for letting us live in his love through acts of random kindness and love that we witness every day.

—J. Winkelmann

✝ ✝ ✝

There's not much time
we've only got one life to live
And it better be right
Full of hope
A hope that teaches how to love
To hold on

To the ones who gave us life
To the little things that open our eyes
To the people that we see everyday
Don't let it slip away
Hold on

—Adam Bitter, "Hold On"
© 2007, Adam Bitter

Rushing from one thing to the next,
from practices to meetings and
from games to classes,
homework, chores, volunteering,
and spending time with friends.
Always on the go!
God, even with a very busy schedule,
help us to take a minute each day to slow down
and enjoy all that you have given us.
When life becomes stressful,
help us to remember what is truly important.
Keep us smiling, laughing, and enjoying life
and all you have to offer.
Amen.

—L. Wiegmann

"The steadfast love of the Lord never ceases,
    his mercies never come to an end;
they are new every morning;
    great is your faithfulness.
'The Lord is my portion,' says my soul,
    'therefore I will hope in him.'"

—Lamentations 3:22–24

thank you, my king, for leading me back to you!

—J. Ecle

† † †

teach us, o Lord

o Lord, teach us to become
truthful students in your class of life.
    Help us to think of you as the fireman
who will save us from the flames of hell.
    Love us as a mother loves her children.
    Forgive us as often and as lovingly
as a true best friend.
    Be the soldier who has our back
in the endless battle against sin and satan.
    our lives are like walking barefoot
on a rocky path. Be our shoes and
help us continue walking.
    Truly, you are our teacher, our fireman,
and our mother. You are our best friend,
our soldier, and our shoes.
    In one day, you are all these and more
to millions, but we ask one more thing of you.
    show us how to do all these things.

—Z. Bormann

Heavenly Father, let your love be the only thing
that drives me and motivates me this day. Let
each of my actions reflect the desire to act in
accordance with your grace.

Lord, your love is better than life. Help me to
know that your love far exceeds any trials,
temptations, or struggles that I may have
throughout the course of this day. In each
moment, and at the end of this day, help me
to know your love and embrace you above all
things.

—A. Young

† † †

"But the Advocate, the Holy Spirit,
whom the Father will send in my name,
will teach you everything,
and remind you of all that I have said to you.
Peace, I leave with you; my peace I give to you.
I do not give to you as the world gives.
Do not let your hearts be troubled,
and do not let them be afraid."

—John 14:26-27

Fully Alive

Camping up in the Rocky Mountains of Colorado was a place I knew I could answer God's call to living fully in his presence. God constantly revealed himself to me, fully alive, in the faith-based community surrounding me and in the beauty of his creation on my way to a summer youth conference in Denver. His presence could be felt in everything from waking up each morning, hearing the peacefulness of the rushing river, to seeing the sunrise come up over the mountains as the earth began to come alive in the morning. Spending those days developing that community of life with God was so important as well, just enjoying the time away from daily distractions. These summer retreats made me feel as if I was coming alive—truly alive. I was able to experience God purely; there was nothing taking me away from diving into his presence and worshipping him with all that I am.

Being fully alive in those retreat experiences is great and sometimes even easy, but God calls us to live fully in him during more than just those times. He calls us out of the experiences of our everyday lives, out of the comfort we build for ourselves. Pope Benedict XVI said it best when he said, "The ways of the Lord are not comfortable, but we were not created for comfort—but for greatness, for good." Living fully in God is our call to greatness! That is our call to more! Living fully involves pursuing a true, personal relationship with Christ through prayer, meditation, and experiencing his love and grace. It is not being content with just "getting by" in faith. Living fully means having a deep longing in your heart that translates into giving of ourselves completely to his will. It is seeking the Lord out in the everyday moments of our lives, knowing that without him we wouldn't be able to do anything. The more fully alive we are, the more we lose ourselves in love with him.

Living fully involves choosing love, choosing prayer, choosing every day to dive deeper into the love that is our God. Living fully is a choice. It is a calling, a calling that involves acting upon the things we believe in our hearts that you know are true because they come from Christ. Being fully alive is letting go of control, knowing that he never lets go, and offering up your life to allow him to move and inspire your actions.

This section contains prayers that show people's hearts at times when they have been on fire for the Holy Spirit and really living (or striving to live) in his presence with their actions. Use these prayers to help you ask God

for the grace necessary to live your life fully in
his presence. we are called to greatness; we are
called to more in our lives. we must be willing
to pray and ask god to help us answer, to choose,
that calling.

"I came that they may have life,
and have it abundantly."
—john 10:10

—peter Higbie

Heavenly Father, my God and Savior,
thank you for hearing my cries and
showing me your unending love.
Thank you for showing me how to serve you,
and how to help others as well.
Thank you for being so merciful and forgiving.
Thank you for all the wondrous blessings
you have so willingly poured out to me.
Thank you for always being with me
and never abandoning me,
even when I doubt.
Thank you for my family, Lord,
and may we walk in your light forever.
Thank you for opening my heart
so that I could see
the way, the Truth, and the Life.
And most of all, Lord,
thank you for giving me eternal life
by dying on the cross.
Amen.

—K. Krekeler

o dear god, forever i will praise
the holy sound
of your gracious name!
you died for our sins,
rose up from the grave.
forever i will praise
your most holy name!
you created the birds of the sky.
you created the fish of the sea.
everything i see
was created by you alone.
almighty god, you watch over us
from your holy throne!
i will trust you forever.
i trust your holy will.
you are the one who makes my heart whole.
you are the one who completes my soul!
amen.

—l. land

I am so full
of those foolish things
we call memories
And I can't control
the desires for which I live and breathe
And I am alone
struggling in the midst of a crashing sea
But then – it's only me

we have got to realize
that the petty prizes that
we name our lives
are not the key to happiness
and fulfilling dreams
For "I" am alone
And "I" am a soul
And "I" can only care about me

But if I give myself up to Jesus
But if I let go of what I think is me
But if we could only see
that just "I" don't mean anything
unless you are all of me

"I" - what a silly little word
it has defined my life
and I let it do so
but I am discovering
that efforts to only make me happy
are not what they were before

Because I have given myself to christ
And he's torn down the mess of me
planted love in my heart and pulled
out all the weeds
and like a mustard seed it grows
taking over everything
until I forget to be me

I never realized that on this crazy journey
I would really lose my life
I thought it meant loving God and others
not dying and rising in christ

But if I give myself up to Jesus
but if I let go of what I think is me
But if we could only see
That just "I" don't mean anything
Unless you are all of me...

—E. wicks, "Unless you're All of Me"

your plans for me are greater than I know,
and stretch farther than I can ever imagine.
Take me and let thy will be done!

—L Halfmann

✝ ✝ ✝

Not to us, O Lord, not to us,
but to your name give glory,
for the sake of your steadfast love
and your faithfulness.

—Psalm 115:1

when your own nothingness combines with the fullness of God, God no longer exists in your presence; you exist in God's presence, fully and wholly in Christ.

—J. Blidy

✝ ✝ ✝

"I ask not only on behalf of these, but also on behalf of those who will believe in me through their word, that they may all be one. As you, Father, are in me and I am in you, may they also be in us, so that the world may believe that you have sent me. The glory that you have given me I have given them, so that they may be one, as we are one, I in them and you in me, that they may become completely one, so that the world may know that you have sent me and have loved them even as you have loved me. Father, I desire that those also, whom you have given me, may be with me where I am, to see my glory, which you have given me because you loved me before the foundation of the world.

"Righteous Father, the world does not know you, but I know you; and these know that you have sent me. I made your name known to them, and I will make it known, so that the love with which you have loved me may be in them, and I in them."

—John 17:20–26

Dear Jesus,
Here in your presence
let everything else fall away
Let me just take a breath
and take a step back

Loving Jesus
here in your presence
you love me as you loved me from the cross
Let your love fill up my life
and radiate through me

Precious Jesus
Here in your presence
we are hand in hand, face to face
I take courage because with you
I am never alone

Beautiful Jesus
here in your presence
you understand me
you love me
and you believe in me

—J. Gillam

you

your warm presence fills my core
like a fire burning in my soul.
your eyes bore into me, yearning for love;
you baffle me with your mindset.
 why doesn't everyone love you?

—c. jump

† † †

i know this place.
it is near to my heart.
here, it is just me,
me and god.

i talk to him
because he always listens.
but it is even better
when i listen.

i lie here,
at peace in my world,
and just let god talk.
god, my friend.

—s. blackwell

O Lord!
Make me a child,
so I may fully believe in you.

Make me a warrior,
so I may fight in your name against evil
in all its forms.

Make me a vessel,
so I may be filled with your Holy spirit
wherever I go.

Make me a servant,
so I can serve you in all ways.

Make me a mirror,
so I may reflect your light to all I see.

Make me nothing,
so I may learn to hold all others above me.

Make me crippled,
so I may learn I can do nothing without you.

Make me shameless,
so I may praise and worship
with reckless abandon!

Make me a saint,
so I may be with you in heaven!

A cry for change from your loving child.

—N. Ciavarra

The gifts he gave were that some would be apostles, some prophets, some evangelists, some pastors and teachers, to equip the saints for the work of ministry, for building up the body of Christ...But speaking the truth in love, we must grow up in every way into him who is the head, into Christ, from whom the whole body, joined and knit together by every ligament with which it is equipped, as each part is working properly, promotes the body's growth in building itself up in love.

–Ephesians 4:11–12, 15–16

our Father, who art in Heaven, hallowed be thy Name	Daddy, you care for us as your children. You are worthy of all my praise and all I am. I love you, Lord, with all my heart, all my mind, and all my soul.
Thy kingdom come	Lord, I want this world to be like you want it to be. Please bless all who don't believe in you, that they may come to see what they're missing and learn to live in your love. Please work in the hearts of all those who contribute to things that plague the world, like abortion and wars.
Thy will be done	Lord, I know that you know what you're doing a whole lot better than I do. Please help me learn to let go and trust in your plan for me, even when I can't see how it's going to work out or feel like my idea sounds better.

on earth as it is in Heaven	Lord, bring the world closer to heaven. I know that through the communion of saints, all the souls with you in heaven are praying for those here on earth. Dear saints, please keep me and my petitions in your prayers.
Give us this day our daily bread	Lord God, I can't do this by myself. I need so much from you. Please give me your divine help in all the struggles I am facing. Graciously grant me whatever it is that you know I truly need in this life.
And forgive us our trespasses	Lord, you and I both know that I mess up — a lot sometimes. I am so sorry for anything I have done that you don't like. Please forgive me. If there is anything I've done to displease you for which I'm not truly sorry, please help me with that so that I may truly be forgiven.

As we forgive those who trespass against us	Lord, it's so hard sometimes to forgive other people. Please grant me your ability to love the sinner while hating the sin. Help me to see the people who have hurt me as people, without first seeing the wrong they have done me.
And lead us not into temptation, but deliver us from evil.	Lord, I am so weak. Grant me your strength and courage to overcome the temptations I encounter, great and small. Help me always to choose the way that leads to you.
Amen.	I love you, Daddy. Please don't let my prayer end here, but let it carry on into my daily life. —C. Attewell

you are my god, my savior...my love, my life,
my salvation, my soul, my spirit and
my unshakable strength, my Lord, my King,
and my best friend, my constant hope,
my unfailing shepherd, my song of joy.

I love you!

—E. wicks

Father God, your love is all I need. Lord, help me to open my heart to you, and fill the cracks with your never-ending love. Jesus, be with me, and help me through this life so I might rejoice with you forever. No matter what happens, Lord, be with me, be by my side. When I laugh, Lord, laugh with me. When I cry, hold me close and wipe away my tears. Jesus, you are all I need, you are all I want. Jesus, come, come into my life. Give me the strength to live my life for you. Send your Holy Spirit to guide me when I stray from the path. Thank you for creating me, always loving me, and for dying for me. I am so grateful for your unconditional and everlasting love.

—K. Hayes

The Lord is my strength and my shield;
    in him my heart trusts;
so I am helped, and my heart exults,
    and with my song I give thanks to him.

—Psalm 28:7

Holy spirit, fill me with the love of christ.
Holy spirit, be with me in all that I do every day,
to aim for your holiness.
Holy spirit, help me to be holier
in my thoughts and in my actions.
Holy spirit, guide me to love and
protect all that is holy.
Please, Holy spirit, be with me every day
and make me holy like you.

Amen.

—V. Halfmann

† † †

*"For through the Spirit, by faith, we eagerly
await for the hope of righteousness."*

—Galatians 5:5

prayer to the holy spirit

come, o holy spirit!
enlighten my mind to know your commands;
strengthen my heart against
    the snares of the enemy;
inflame my will...
i have heard your voice,
and i don't want to harden myself and resist,
saying "later... tomorrow."

nunc coepi! now i begin!
in case there is no tomorrow for me.

o spirit of truth and wisdom,
spirit of understanding and counsel,
spirit of joy and peace!
i want whatever you want.
i want because you want,
i want however you want,
i want whenever you want.

—st. josemaria escriva

Praise be to God, king of heaven and earth!
My soul longs to praise you forever!

—J. Ecle

† † †

Lord God, help me to always know that you are
my source of life. Reveal to me, more and more
each day, what it truly means to be dependent
on you.

Heavenly Father, your power is made perfect
in my weakness. Help me to abandon my pride
at your feet, and allow your meek and humble
heart to transform my own heart.

Lord Jesus, I desire wholeheartedly that your
will may be accomplished in my life; I give you
permission to change anything and everything in
my life that does not give you praise.

—A. Young

Lord,

you are my everything. you pick me up when
I have fallen; you carry me when I am down.
you are my castle and my strength, my protector
and savior. Lord, I come to you with a plea for
forgiveness, and a desire to follow you. I give
my life and my soul to you, and ask that you
would take me and shape me to your will.
Lord, you are my rock to stand on when I am
weak and the one I glorify when I am strong.
Help me to be one with you.

Amen.

—C. Jones

"Bring me the sunset in a cup"
That I may drink and be filled up
with light and love and beauty true
For all I am and all I do

Give me the purity of the rain
To cleanse me through and heal my pain
To wash away all hurt and sin
That I've done and that I'm in

Grant me the diamond-studded sky
The peace of stars my heart let fly
For strength and fire within my soul
To warm me through and make me whole

Show me the glory of the sea
And I shall dance of joy in Thee
waves will crest like glass and I
will flow with praise of God on high

—C. Attewell

(The first line of this prayer comes from a poem
by Emily Dickinson of the same name.)

Let the heavens be glad, and let the earth rejoice;
let the sea roar, and all that fills it;
Let the field exult and everything in it.
Then shall all the trees of the forest sing for joy
before the Lord: for he is coming,
for he is coming to judge the earth,

He will judge the world with righteousness,
and the peoples with his truth.

—psalm 96:11–13

your love is amazing.
Lately, its unconditional nature
perplexes and warms me.
I cannot comprehend
how much you infinitely love me!
sometimes I catch a glimpse of it
and I sigh in joy. I am so little, Lord.
why do you love me?

—E. wicks

"I speak these things in the world
so that they may have my joy
made complete in themselves...
that the world may know that
you have sent me and have loved
them even as you have loved me."

—John 17:13, 23